BEHIND THE NIGHT

Published by Dan Burke

Printed in the United Kingdom.

To
Mel

BEHIND THE NIGHT

DAN BURKE

Enjoy the read
darling
Dan x.

John Daniel Burke is an unknown poet from the west side of the City of Newcastle upon Tyne. He is influenced by Jim Morrison, *The Doors* lead singer. He was born in October 1974. He was brought up by his mother and step-father and has two brothers. His biological father died before he was born. He attended Rutherford Comprehensive and Newcastle College. His other main influences are Arthur Rimbaud and Charles Baudalaire.

This book is for family and friends no longer with us. To friends and family still here. And to the ones who are yet to come.

Contents

I. Behind The Night

II. Shadows of the Past

Introduction

We are all collectors
Envious in our hording
Our shallow baseness
Makes us feel we're falling

So in swift movements
We bewilder ourselves
Mechanical in the stream of certainty

An Hour By Hour Revolution

An hour by hour revolution is, more or less, a following of oneself and a disregard for all barriers. Trust in your own premonitions and believe firmly of your road. A constant digging and overturning of your field- but most importantly, to be able to carry it through, using your shape, voice, and your greatest wisdom; which is action.

The Moon

I feel you staring through me
Dry blooded Cynthia
Serenading the tide
Locked against the night

I feel you staring through me
My incipient bride
Your hypnotic unfading gaze
Cools my curious face

I feel you staring through me
Hanging over the hills
This voyeuristic chill
Has claimed me

I feel you drawing me in
Your patient wisdom dreamt me
From the blackness of the past
Sunlight turned hallow as you went on past

The Night

O the night

What do you hold away from my behest?
I plan to touch you, the untouchable breast
Hidden behind garments-
How I need your caress

I cannot sleep, but still I cannot kiss you
Why does everything have to become such an issue?
Prayers in the gallows when I cannot reach you
Seeking in the light your brilliant face

So I imagine on this sullen path, the growing force of your finery
Unmistakeable beauty smiling without the sun
So I shall obtain the mysteriousness of you, if my time
Reaches to you; for the remembrance of a name

Goodbye, until we meet again.

Black n' Sprawling Sea

O black and sprawling sea
You terrify me
Still I don't want you to die
Even in the womb we say goodbye

For my life just hovers
Above the realness of me
Hiding the darkest depths
The deepness of the sea

If I let go, it would shatter
Which I hold to fast-

The subscript of time
Brought to ground
By the naturalness of crime

The Insane

I have heard the screams of the impotent men
I have watched their bodies writhe in hell
Burning skin rose up as smoke
Scenting their nostrils, while clogging their throats

Bitter tears well up into their eyes
Acid rain streaming, from the sullen skies.
Pores wide open to the feverish pain
Remorse echoes their mind to remove blood stains.

This boat set sail on the river, alone
Shuddering, stuttering almost broke.
Peace in solace to forget the game
Broken shells by a dying flame

For visions are repressed in pulsating scenes
Alone in the room w/deaths rising scream
Vibrating views of life as natural crime
Rat ridden streets in heavy time

Broadmoor

The mirror is dependant, and depending on the eyes
Hear the workings of the buried mind
Way beyond the haze and the blinding sun
The insane come

Carving out of stone their deathly shapes
Trying to be one, when it's too late
Wanting to fill the void of a vacant skull
The slaughter house resembles perfect love

When grazing in the corridors of sin
Eternally innocent of everything
Always on the verge of impossible light
They dwell in the night

So the blood flows in pity and
The demons of their pain
Takes a foot over the edge, smelling at the grave
To die in bitter rivers, or in fires of rage

Gothic Was His Look

Gothic was his look
of terror
hooded was his head
and eyes
Of soft madness creeping through
To stare and seize a hold of you

Hypnotised as the snake controls
To have its way by streams of gold
Inclines the prey to (utterly) give
Its life for peace

Germs of death born in
The womb
Placed on a stage for sorry fools
To play dice for a hollow throne
This can't compare to what will come

The strength of the folk from
The old world
Will paint purple this shallow globe
The comfortable haunts all
Crumbled and burned
As Wotan appears from his darkened urn

Can you not hear his growing footsteps
in the cellar?
The volcano erupts and the red hot lava
Deems that chaos is the life that we stand in
As madness reaches all on its burning chariot

The grass is raging
w/ fire
and devils appear to quiet Christ's choir
Church and steeple cleared of all the dust
Healthy air blows all signs of rust

We clear our throats?
We wipe the scars of mind?
To look ahead w/ bright wide open eyes!

Cool damp dew has quenched thirsty revenge

He heads back to his cave
Then begins his march again

The Quality Of Purple

The quality of purple-
Calm, magic splendour.
A dark Angel.
The edge of a grave.
The midnight face.

My woman is older.
Her electric eyes bring thought to neon light
She has become colder
Her vision is in sight

Ancient spirit of man-
Evolves, revolves;
Bewitching the skull
The mind stings w/ the sight of blood

We sharpened knives on each other-
love

The Network

Hedonistic destiny
Whispering warm thought breath
Into destiny

Modern man;
The desperate chance
Improvements?
Our sullen godly image

Tragic deformities-

Then science
Then religion
Never ending arguments and guilt

Hereditary rings-
Can they be untied?

Science; genius of progression
Demon minds, dark nous

Thick roots of morality
Ancient dust of night
Break the despisers
Jealous of flight

Transcendental

Rise sun
Fire world

I'm slayer of the stars
I'm healer of the heart
Shed light through corners of secrecy

II

(Obedient jets pierce the sky in readiness for the profit war)
The truth won't change, just hide.
Conspiracy wastes and twists into lies.

`So very well, fall in love w/the gun`
Sacrificial blood drops stain the reflections of the sun

We are tied into network, w/cops as surgical soldiers.
The Middle East as arena.
The gamble for humanity is on

III

Will identity crises ever be settled?
Will paranoid fanatics ever lose their cold death lust?
We begrudge the wind its cold sensation
Huddled together, comfortable in our caves
w/modern luxury

T.V. is a contaminating cancer

The international arena formed into one little box trap
Immense in its range to confuse the skull

Change equals hostility.
Great opposition
A game until the end

Forced change
Contradiction, shudder and shake
Awake!
Take a bow through time
Life begins w/a scream-
The darkness mixed w/ mother gleam

Reflections in the extreme.

Our cool Universe-
In solitude
Night brings Light

Heroin

The brown leaves him plenty of
Room to decide
The moon slips away in
Sulky recline
The body is prostrate in
A silent room
Monstrous shadows rise
Into the gloom

Trying to palliate their
Unwanted zeal
Will this numb repose
Really heal?
Well it has been recommended!
He only dreams of
The woman who said this
On his-

Dream boat;
Wish boat
Slide across the steam
The quintessence of disease
Is a concupiscent must-
Realised, w/a magnificent thrust.
Love- love- love. Pain- pain- pain
Will we ever wake up again?

The Overdose

Remember the suave companion?
The curtain of every scene
Is your boat at peace on the stream?
Followed, for he will not leave
An untenable whisper- luxury!

Like a mistress untangling what seems
Wondering onto a strangers' field
To remember
What will not be born or past?
Untenable! An eternal fast

Bring back the old forms
I can't recognise this face
The body on the cross seems out of place
Look through the mist, there, on the periphery is a stage
I'm going. I'm late

It Coils...

It coils, universal unconscious snake
Around drug beaming essence of my eyes
To drag through my memory
Like a poisoned slug
Harsh w/ its fever
When stealing my love

Buttoned safely w/sleep now
In the great shadows of the dream
Swathed, a mysterious boat on a stream
The sumptuous lather steals
Into the groves of the brain

As the moon slides on
Curious utopian run
To magnetise space for the mother
The sun

O, but then the lightning-
Dogs barking, invade
The silent maw of our soft escape

The Painful Game

The painful Game
Drawing in
My brain

Is crowding my
Nights
w/sorrowful sights

The storm
Is my life

Socrates

Socrates, ah socrates
Our lives are generated by causality?

Existentialism
The void.

Once its over its over
(it doesn't take very long to be forgotten)

We have to digest all that is hard to digest

Could all our hard work be for nothing?
Swallow your view

Every thing is constant
Time lurks like an existent ghost

Keep on digesting
Man
You'll be your own saviour

Boredom ignites danger

Oh Universe

Oh Universe is so sad that I cried
The stars that used to give us hope
Have died

Time in reverse
I'm alive in a hearse

Every thing is that
It's opposite
And everything else

I'm Alive
I'm Dying

Neurosis

Can you hear the hollow
Reflecting

Sound of time, behind
The night

Content and cool-
Although a little on edge.

Senses aware of this creeping
Fear hysteria.

Lodged in the backwoods of
Your mind
That summer security has left you-

As the moon looks on in pity
At your lost bravado

The Blind

Your silent quivering
In days you cannot mock
Dignified bewilderment
Is shallow, is it not?

Onto the swirling night –
No more mysterious than the day
Into the realm of dreams
This mind will rush and stray

Then curse the echoing voices
Delve into the memories stream
Straining w/desire, and
Deafened by the scream;

Of former days of colour
Haunting you like a ghost
What is the time?
I think you've seen enough

The Battle of Minds

The battle for minds has begun
In the church and in the home
T.v. and where the movie runs
Watching plays and freak shows

Preach and subtle altered tones
Osmosis, cerebral slowed and pause.
Into the blood stream
Then the bones

The Priest

You arrived on this world
To set yourself apart
From the vulgarity of the masses
And the weakness of their hearts

As you stole into their dreams
Waving your golden key
The glow of heaven is not of earth?
Well MY god may disagree

So life forms, evolving now
Across the sunlight, they have many shapes
Imply the voice heard from the cross
Is the freedom of the snake?

So I point my finger now,
Into your eyes of pity
Jumping from your lustful dearth
Into the bosom of the city

The Crusade

You wanna be a statue
Of circus blunder
Cool marble Mohammed
Dying restless w/herd crowd plunder

Fall by the wayside-

Tradition in the veins
The madness of the past
Strays careless in our brains

Death coloured leaves
War, barbed wire trees-
Silk gloves will not save
Your son

God is a false war mongering whore

Abortion

Bring back the umbilical less spirit
It was felled from the back of the world
Falling down every tunnel
On fire it's poor little soul

Screams creep into the nightmare
Blood is dripping from the flower
All for lack of consonance
The smiling constrictor is dour

So blessings to you, fertility
Seeds flow in murderous waves?
A curious desire to know you
Put features on an empty face

Paradox Of Hope

We were doing nothing
Then I was gone
In the midnight drawer
Of silent scope
The aching thought that we
Were all lost
Tested the faith
In hope

Then lightning blazed
And tore the sky
A glimpse of the gods
In wanton minds
They stirred to open
Just one eye
As if afraid they were
Going to die

But the Pentecost spirit who
Arrives at birth
Showed them the paradox
Of hope
That those who have vision
Will die
And those with no wings
Will fly

Save us!

Immortal Hand

A blaze in the sky, a messenger of light
Through the darkness of the night
What warm immortal hand
Granted infinity to the shore and sand?

What raging life force was it that brought sun into the sky?
That gave the wind its whistle?
That gave the moon its sad goodbye?
The shore a whispered hush, for autumns golden rush

Then what finger was it? It carried thunderbolts
Through this planetary temptress of time
To bless our minds w/sight and vision
Keeping alive thoughts of the divine

For here, where the air does fill our lungs
We have angels caressing our minds
And when our hopes would be extinguished
How could it be in this life which is mine?

For the fog and the chill will not freeze our sturdy hearts
Will not blanket the sea on the day we do depart
For the clock of the land will not devour the immortal hand
In this life of ours, in this life

Pickpocket The Moon

Pick pocket the moon
Then swallow the sun
I bleed
As the sorrow of the night concedes

Dust from space
Upon our face

Weighed down w/the boredom
This monotony you have created
Put down your cigarette holder
Take off your gloves
We have anticipated-

Your hallow screams
Your breathless dreams
Head on your course across the pure ancient night-

O and do not take flight

For yes we all have our fantasies
Our hopes it seems
Let us not spoil them w/the truth

I Stand

I stand and fix a stare
Deluge of my body
Scaffold around the veins
A statue for the pain

My eyes absorb the mirror
Exterior- Osmosis- Interior

Plants, aliment decay
The night swallows the day

Rhythm of sexual motion
Freedom was killed by emotion
Our bodies are bound to contain
Fearful energy under electric sway

Skin peels off and dies
The brain is sucked into the maggot's eye
Fed to the elements of earth
Eternal death and rebirth

The Top

Fancy worrying about what we have not got
To stretch the ego
Do not stamp it under foot

Help us understand the luminescence of the dawn
What was it like?
Man; the forest lived before

O violent hand, does it really reach the stars?
Do our religious depths
Bring on the dance?

For music's hypnotic trance
A soldier marching
The west has been advanced

Thunderous tanks of steel in a desert
Business deals of blood turned green
So shall we dare ask ourselves

Is the fire really real?
Did our sons come on home last night?
Was he slumped upon evil deeds?

Poppy seeds and oil fields!
Vomit across the political walls!
The lords are badder than they ever where before

You can reach the top my brother!
But only if you learn to crawl

The Riot

We were drenched in blood

My mind became a fallen temple
Of adrenalin and fear

He lay there dying- the riot progressed
Onto a plane of fire
As eruption pressed

Glass is flying.

Skulls are crushed.

'O, sorry son, it stays the same'

The fool thought it wasn't just a game

The man knew.

On his porch, smoking time

A wry smile

Very Fitting Indeed

Very fitting indeed it is
When mortals hug together
Smiling, waving upon a breeze
Oblivious of bad weather

The movement of infinity took strength
Fate is a diamond lodged into the brain

His fate
His brain

Faith is something that
Can't be bought
Faith is pain that
Can't be taught
Faith is a long, lone
Winter ride
Faith belongs in the
Immortal tide

The gods smiled
We laughed at the world
We love the gods

The homogenous stones
Burned down a creators world

The parade goes marching on
W/out knowing what it walks upon

The hero takes a chance
Shows the universal how to live
Romance

He died.
He couldn't survive the tremors
The horrors
The strains of the tide

Immerse w/the body for the sake of soul
The windows are open-
Freedom rides home

Dramatic dance
Devouring fear. Reabsorbed
into crystal
Converged w/our prayers

Do not tremble my good friend
Give your senses leave
Wearing your heart as the body
Impulses on the sleeve

The long, mad corridors w/marble rooms
Sink into sleep now- it may do you good

Drift on in the nightmare
Stare out far, don't drawn
They say your wet mind, your disease
Shook up the town

Prostrate across the covers
Black and blue and your shallow ribs
Broken buried w/invisible sin

Hallucinations

Confrontations
[The knife is drawn to kill the run of the mill]

A part of me can see, a part which will not laugh
The laughing part takes of its hat, to wipe the blood
Spilled on the mat
Get me out of this room
Where do I belong?
Its no use me staying here, I'm too ill to choke

Choke upon your memories
I can feel your melting mind
Wipe it clean w/stronger pills
Take it from the night

Involutedly, the night complains of
Diseased species that crawl on its side
Lechery is born here
Lechery is its bride

It belongs in the shadows?
It belongs in the light!
The gaze of the darkness
Lets it grow in height

Hovering in doorways
A dear old maid
Make sweet my collar
£ 20 love street parade

They have been reborn it seems
In your regular hotel
Hanging from your worn out nipples
Blinded from your cares

It now becomes a fact to me
The pollution of my soul
Let me sense purity
Please girl take me home!

Lengthy quotes from the bible
Doug on the monument stage
"Sorry Doug I'm already lost"
Lucifer's in my brain

Lost on the edge of a whirlwind
A Midnight crying scream
Emaciated by the haughty night
w/ nothing left but dreams

The More You Let Yesterday Affect You

The quicker future dies

The Venerable Muse

I open you and immediately do I find
The particles of freedom for the mind.
Like jewels they come, to lodge where we can see
Then before they go I grip them tightly

It is summer dazzling, shining through our hair
The pond that reflects our heavenly lair
A woman smiling, gladdened wantonly
You are the wizened goddess of mystery

Can't fathom you the breaker of the chains
The moon, the sun, and rainbow of its rays
You keeper of the fort who holds the keys

The description of the leaves upon the trees
A genius of progression and the heart
A whisper in the night beyond the stars

Rimbaud

My life is lead through a...
A basic hypnosis-
And chaos
Into the realms of art
The eye of vision expands the world

This life does flow, through
Haunting caverns
I shall rest like the lion
At the end of the labyrinth
People are blessed who laugh when it's done

My arrow must rise, to strike past nostalgia
Turning convictions into stone
Hear it soundly
Our futuristic home

Which life stands alone?
A unique emblem

There is a rumour of peace
At the end of the arrow
A rumour of violence
In the conception of time
A true rumour
In the soft lie

The Whore

I lied to you because you were born
A crumbling ship that rests on timeless shores
An attempt that has been burned by the sun
A grave that has always been dug

You belong to corrupted demons, never fair
For a glass of wine or stale bottle of beer
And your future dies inside your dirty trap
A ragged damsel riddled w/the clap

An unashamed hypocritical bitch
You're only happy when you're getting whipped
A silent complicity w/your ugly masters
They hang their skeletons in the worst of cupboards

So here, inside the lonely night again
W/diseased smiles they queue outside your den
You swallow them in haste like quickened fever
So you can't be quenched by the phallus lever

Then come, you hag, smooth prostrate queen
Collaborate w/the old mans dreams
I know you don't expect, so just see
That you blossom from the roots of what you feel

The Venal Broad

O you fickle dainty butterfly
Too quick to flight for the sunless mass,
While I brood on dimensions of the soul
Deeper than the very depths of being

You are as elusive as my spectre at night
That before the morning star does gleam
Silently drifts back to the past
Leaves me lost in the reality of the dream

For I want to grip you, to breathe your scent,
And extinguish my frustrated woes
To keep sullen improbity in check
Worship you through your body and soul

But still you dazzling firebrand,
Are naïve to my onrushing blaze?
I'll pluck you, to water my desert
Then coalesce in the river of change

She Is My Girl

She is my girl
Needs me
as fire

Obsolete

Tears

Desire

(Wine soaked mind
Drying out
Wished her away)

Forget

Forgotten,
and past

Mitigates the future at last

Impression Of Beauty

O beauty, how you rise to overtake the sun
You reflect in me the joys of perfect love
But when you scorn, your stare can freeze a heart
The earth stops breathing when we are apart

My senses dulled, I am alone at sea
The heavens open, firing thunderbolts
A wreckage heading straight towards the rocks
I'm crucified; I'm bleeding on the cross

Then w/a sudden smile the chains are broken
A path withing life's tall mystery
So the eternal master over me
Has infinity and beauty as my tokens

So I honed and pruned her delicacy there
To guard from the troubles her secret cares
Velvet in the slipstream of her private prayers

Baudalaire

Apathy yawns, digs

Crawls, slides-
To impose and to bolster
Fanciful sleep

Hovering, sucking the mind dry

For ennui and sorrow to greet

We have an intense capacity
For suffering
While we evolve into an ideal-

The body is writhing in agony
Attacked by the darkness of spleen

She Is Afraid

She is afraid of
My Night

Come
Because we're young

I won't dismantle
Your delicate tongue

See the movie
Run

Visions Of The Past

The night brings me visions of the past
In a city with all its sultry charms
Born of yesterday- mists hovering across the moody river
Soft light echoing upon an ancient steeple

The spirit from decades ago
The other generations and the lost side show

The eternal beat of the church bell
Hallowing in my soul one million farewells
As the eye dwells upon the horizon
In sinewy with the dream and more

Pulsating through me to enter my mind
Infinitely I love for ever more

Born in me a tear of sadness
Goodbye to the ones that lived before
Fragmented in the awkward day
Our holy sullenness deviates we stay

Life What Are You But A Brief Audition

Life what are you
But a brief Audition

And could it be
No one ever GETS
The part

Waiting For God

Come to me in the languid groaning
Of the breeze
Come to me in the sweet humming
Of the day
Come to me in the dour oblivion
Of decay
Come to me in the perspiration song
Of pain

Come to me in the silent repose
Of the night
Come to me as the great essence
Of the dream
Come to me as the face in
Fires bright
Come to me as wicked love my
Dearest queen

Come to me in the crying echo
Of the valley
Come to me in the haunting forests
Of the fields
Come to me in the dusty desert
Of silence
Come to me in the noise
Of futile screams

Come.

Death

Time, the slow hooded craftsman
Creeping into consciousness, sliding
Through our bones
Like corrupted piety, for corroded idle souls

Enter the slip of the undergrowth
Parched in a shrouded way
Broad anaconda on our path-
So in the darkness we pray

For quietly stealing breath
Punctilious master of the dark
Bringing to ground our mortal span
W/vulgar eyes for the clock

Then the overfriendly hand
Rises frostily from the deep –
Ghost angel on the wing whispers
'Your turn for eternal sleep.'

Shadows of the Past

Hallow is the empty tomb

Hallow is the empty tomb
When madness creeps into the room
The ghostly faces
Crawl the walls this side

Infinity flashes before us
Then kills us from behind

What of this place we live on?
So sullen and deep

Other than to be born
To live
Then fuck off to sleep

Buckingham St

Hallow space was-
The echo of the brewery

The cats' eyes bite
To haunt the subway

Old Street is gone
The school holds a ghost

Sucked by time
Down the gaping slopes

Convalescence

Not many caverns in the soul
That will bring forward peace
Where are the places for me to dwell?
When I really need to think

Where shadows sway across walls
High wizardry present and magic makes mockery
Of the witnessing sun
Thoughts snatch at invisible signs

Trying to untangle love

For this tunnel is deep and
Its vacuum gauge chills
An illusory trammel
As the dawn is still'd

When up rises a hand
As loneliness melts away
Dwelling in eternity
Smiling at the awkward day

Fatherhood

O.K. so I'm all shaved and wash'd up
Then for what reason is it to grow a beard?
For a long and drawn out futile life!

No, it is this-

To live for your child or children
And their broadest grin
Wider than the sun

Heaven is Close Up

Heaven is close up
In the Northumberland fields
Entering the soul
A vast ship w/sails

Reaches into your mind
The hearts eternal friend
Languidly steals your breath
And then-

You cannot grasp it
Beauty is a far out thing
It bursts onto your life
Like infinite rain

Listen Here Now

Listen here now!
The comet comes
A centuries worth of light years
But it's heading for our world!

Swift gliding decay
Burning out by the infinite shore
Stars shriek then watch it pass
Far out insect eyes connect it to glass

Light a cigarette
Watch the fire
Calm drawn out time
Beside the flame

A Small Part Of Power

A small part of power
A gliding shadow on an hour
A blink in the descending
Of the sun

What is supposed to happen will come
Your movie has not yet started to run
And when you're young
Don't fall my son

The stars in the night still shine
Even when we're not here
Or we're dying

All is you can do is live it full.
I'm not lying
I'm flying

Night

Night-
Haunting blackness
Thunder and rain

A terrifying connection of
Sound

Through the centre of the brain

The madman in the phone booth-
Storm
Lives in fatuous need

Wanting me out there
To indulge the disease

Black crombie jacket
Stained leather gloves

His eyes shine knowing
(a cold flowing soul)

A hovering hate

Bring out the gun-
Before it's too late

Remember The Handshakes

Remember the handshakes
At times there was even fun
Now all we have is poison
All we have left is big guns

Come teach me how to laugh
Been miserable for so long
The king snake searches his prey
Through the madness of the day

People walking through shallow light
The body is on strike
Stray through the dark when the experiment is through

Forget the handshakes
I'm coming for you

Plague

It rolls slowly
The clunk of the hooves
Horse

The reeking stench

'Bring out your dead'

Across all villages
The land is black

The flowers have fallen to hell

'Bring out your dead'

Blood breath

Poison bread

Bones

'Bring out your dead!
Bring out your dead!
Bring out your dead!'

Drunk In The Kitchen

The bounds of license all around
Sensitive, bleeding
Emotional buttons

Hard, deep, wicked laughter
Pains in the ribs and stomach
The room
The mood

The edge is near
Comedy changes from open to personal
Steroid bull mans angry blush

The Chase

Speed
Dread
Panic
Turning, whirling
Crashing
Dying

Flowers, they're crying

Cold corpse

Forgave the corpse

Scared to touch,
the unknown touch.
Trembling hands

I know him

You did
It's over

The Dawn Smiles

The Dawn Smiles
Then fiery red and orange fire
Claim the horizon

I wipe last night madness
From strained brain
Feel lean and hallow
In the singing morning

The world is mine
All thoughts now peacefully mine

My life blends into the sky and sea

Second man abroad
The dogs bark
The cars moan

O not these again
I'm going home

They Had To Go, Sadly Away

They had to go, sadly away
Died- to drift home
When the morning breaks
The colours show
Relatives behind their heavenly throne

Orange mountains
Thick, mixed w/red
Purple streaks flood
In subtle tones
Blissful tresses, nostalgic poems

Far away from this world
They hold their smiles
Next to me, by the melting isle.
Their memories do float and sing
Eternity touched w/their beautiful wings

Throw Messages Out

Throw messages out
Towards the future
To chase
To confront and to laugh

To moisten hard ground
W/an unloosening whisper
Wide psychedelic views
And the loveable mystic

The heart swimming on trembling waves
Longing for home in an empty space
Of thunder visions
Upon suppressed dread

Invisible monster
Coiled upon our floundering weakness'
That is really guilt
Fumbling in the dark

We Chase After Gods

We chase after gods
In the life
Of fast quest
For emotional wipe out

In the morning it was calmer
In the morning we were wiser
The night we all were madder
W/feasts and torn out flesh

Give me back my eyes
Bring back my world
Let me into the fields
I fly wildly above

You know what you did?
Made the poor girl run
Sacrificial blood drops stain
The reflections of the sun

I Give You Thoughts For Your Mind To Spend

I give you thoughts for your mind
To spend

On suitcases
And grand farewells

And I give you hope
So your pain is slight

And I give you love
So the hope is bright

Insecurity Don't Buy You The Blues

Insecurity don't buy you the blues

It buys you-

Neurotic states to compete w/fever
Jealous eyes if you cannot see her

Avaricious lust to collect those jewels
A joke a minute as a far out fool

Plant your seed
Watch it grow

In the void
Or in her hole

Jealousy

A whispering smoggy voice
Into the woman's naïve brain
Makes my flesh pale white
And my forest turns to flame

Where a ghost becomes flesh
And its tongue a rising thunder
I fall into an abyss of snakes
Then die from jealousies plunder

To rest in bitterest dust
A curse on my sullen state
That damns my soul to the devil
And blankets w/ice my face

So beyond the lies and dead honesty
In front of my doubting eyes
The suffering was the murder of decency
And nobility has crying eyes

And When We Waited For God To Come

And when we waited for god to come
In the beautiful moonlight
After the setting sun
Our patience ran out, we set our sights on love

What we did not realise
He was already there
In the gorgeous silky tresses of her hair
In the wind that gales in the trees at night

In the lonely dwelling on top of a hill
The devil drank w/us that night

She Did Love Me

She did love me
Yes, she loved me so
With all her flesh, vomit, satire, cheek
And greasy dirt

She wanted to love-
As only she could
Her wiry pride
Strangling her mind

I told her to leave
It was all too much
I told her not to undress
I wasn't good enough

She persisted.
I insisted
No compromise in the lake of disguise

Don't climb there girl
She fell

The Pig Tailed Foreign Whore

The pig tailed foreign whore (sorry)
Laughs behind safe effrontery
Magnetising semen into
Her casual drawer

She walks as in a play or
Acting out film
O you're dying,
Desperately dying

It seems like swift decay
Your heart in a blanket
Eyes turning away
What can I do but laugh?

Sad men cry as you tell your story
Keep their feminine couch
All warm until morning

Winter Woman

You smiled to drop a bomb
This blew up my soul
Then donned the blouse of
A former hell
Nature crushed my mind
W/this drawn out spell

A suitcase full of ashes

Farewell

Woman that part the waves
Then steal the game
W/invisible rope and silent chains
They come, in mask; to put out the flame
Burying the spirit under a rocky stage

So take a deep breath, as she will pass
Like the future in a broken glass
And autumn's leaves are winters repast
I once loved you

But now I leave w/the smile of the summer reborn
A butterfly stung by many thorns

We Have The World

We have the world
We have water and growth
And I feel fine

The cool, hard emptiness
Of caves
Dry sand blows
We wipe our eyes

I am on my own
If I needed saving
Who would save me?

She took me to the cabin on
The edge of the water
We sang songs and
Laughed by a fire

I must leave now
The moon has gone

My Heart And The Text

My heart and the text w/ the
Brain are betwix'd
As sparks are emitted from
My fingertips

Communication through
The phone is enriched
As eye contact becomes
Extinct

I can't physically
Entwine into you
As the buttons become the soul
I type to master you

Earth, wind and fire
As contrast is through
Where technology is God
What the fuck can you do ?

I Roam Because The Known Is Meek Descent

I roam because the known is meek decent
To cherish what is troublesome, unspent
Then strike ice upon the things that are complete
To seek adventure, a fragrance that is sweet

But w/this art we all must have a cave
To brood on treasures collected on the way
For memory may get lost in the deep
Where the smiling wanderer tires to fall asleep

For w/sustained energy, nothing ever falls
And the awakened man again will hear his call
Away from family blood and planted seed
Where sorrow dies new spirit takes the lead

Now demons turn to angels and fear is bold
Our shrinking violets now are standing stern
New birds arrive to sing immortal song
Then paradise, once lost; has been reborn

Build Fences

Build fences
Around lines of
Blood

No tunnels away
From the tyrants glove

His burning eyes
Boil the sea
Work sets you free

Freedom is earned w/a resigned shovel

Electric dream
Divine state
The corpses are eternal

Black and Deep Across the Land

Black and deep across the land
Midnight stars and
Revolutionary bands

Ideas shot from the television
World brain
The day is lost amidst our heavenly word plays

We cannot feel our forefathers' touch
Stuck in modern debauchery and
The life of jealous lust

We dwell on god
In case we want to give up

For our eyes are the vanities of god(s)
Given to glimpse the beauty
Of the stars

This creation and the lives we have to see
May have the power
To set our visions free

All Drawn Out and Dead

All drawn out and
Dead
After the war

Collect your belongings
Place them in a jar

You are bound to get something
For playing your part

The worms are in

The blind mans not

Dwelling for Whispers

Dwelling for whispers
Inside the fields
Fates swift fist
Rising in the breeze

Over the meadows
Into the mire
Arrows of strength
To hold the free

Opaque mind-visionary
Glide w/the dance
Setting the stride
For dignity

Play w/the fire
Of clearer hope
Wipe away
The aroma of smoke

Fear is Absent When You Think of Naked Woman

Fear is absent when you think of naked woman
Dancing through fields of glorious light
Towards the end of spring

Complete familiarity.
Isolated dawn men's fast
The forest is alive
The night is awake
Cloaking the moon w/rich purple silk

Dionysian magic
The supreme blessing
A bowing deity
They killed him

Do we not feel disaster?
Until we see blood
Detached naivety until the axe falls
When the darkness introduces stealth

The Journey

Frost covered, across the horizon
Pale in reflection upon the celestial dawn
Energy frozen and static
Alone, upon a lonely shore

Withered and sad is his cheerful nature.
Her soul imprisoned from wrong ideas.
What can we now think to get up to?
Perhaps from now we never will

In mortal silence.
Into cool whispered pain
To escape into sleep,
Never to rise again

No more of your greetings
No more fancy smiles
The fires are ashes
Dust stains the eyes

Come on time soldier-
We know you can rise again
The wind is howling
The leaves are blowing

Clean out the spirit
Rekindle the fertile fire
I am lost for words
The show needs to go on

You say that you won't finish as you start.
What kind of attitude is this for our children to follow?
Are they to make up their own hell?
'No need Sir. There really is no need. We have seen to all of that'
I know, I witnessed the killings. I witnessed the stabbings and the beatings
Down there on the punished ground
Blood mixed w/dust and glass
Intermingling w/horror

The eyes expand in the darkness
Caressing curiously the stars
Insatiably we gloat
Upon the deathly friction of our existence

Now isn't that curiosity my friend
Isn't that searching?
To glow and be strong in the midst of gloom
To strive after happiness
To be ripe for lighter times

Fun is hard work
Laughter ever still
To expand like the sun
To grow out of distress
Forward march!
Present arms
Take off your uniform and your shining boots
We're going casual
Down beside the sea

Take a break-
Away from the cancer city
Dirty collars, lizard air
Dust cars pale on the narrow road

She loves to drive fast cars
She wears shades and smiles
The wind breezes through her deep magnificent hair

We arrived at the gate come sundown
An ancient old man greets us
His hair cloud white and godly
He is prophet philosopher and scientist and keeper of the castle

The girl is amazed.
We drink wine. Fifty years old
Very potent, very bitter, stolen from France
But very much to our taste

If I had a bottle a day I could relax
Says god
This old man, the pious one is making her nervous
She looks but glances away if their eyes meet
Maybe she wants to fuck him

It is getting cold.
We polish off then head to the car
One hundred and thirty miles per hour
It is getting late.
The moon is riding high and wholesome
The trees stir

Slow down! Take it easy!
I take it to the limit honey-
Over the edge and a little more
Tight bends and steep slopes
Fear touches my tongue
My body vibrates w/the car locked against the road

We are racing the night
The wind withdraws our voices as
We speed back down to the Netherworld

I used to be loved there
In amongst that gazing fearful city
My dawning of dreams
Innocently strolling through its ugly seams

Little Grandma there is no need for eyes
You would not like what you would see
Ancient blood visions w/frightening music
Cuts, stabs and knavish bullets
Blasting karma and rocking our structures
The city is mad, severed and broken

II

I suppose it is possible to have a girl, settle down
I suppose it is possible to have a brand new XK super powered
Monstrously fast, jet arsed motherfucking speed rocket to drive

I suppose it is possible to have a large detached, brilliant white, superbly modern
House on a hill where only friends are allowed past the large dog w/the huge head
But
Will this save your little scrawny arse?

We have to learn a way to let go of these small, false and empty races to happiness
Come on I'll read the future for you
Aim. Aimlessly?

We were led to the back of the house
She is dressed in black
Her arm bands rattle

She searches my palm- for clues of the past
For gems of the future
To tell what will last

Disease go
Sadness leave
Bury badness underneath the tree
Lying low w/ nowhere to go

Life becomes bare
Winters cold breath is here
Time to reflect upon
Sins of summer

The room is quiet, apart from
Low sounding music behind the door
The night reflects the story
Of my soul

Gives light to my dreams
Upon the silver plane
Enchant the mysteries touched
w/a hidden flame

O life
Weaver of complexity
Tension of contradiction
Spirits fortress and guardian

Owner of savage beauty
Set me on my quest

May I return fulfilled and do you justice